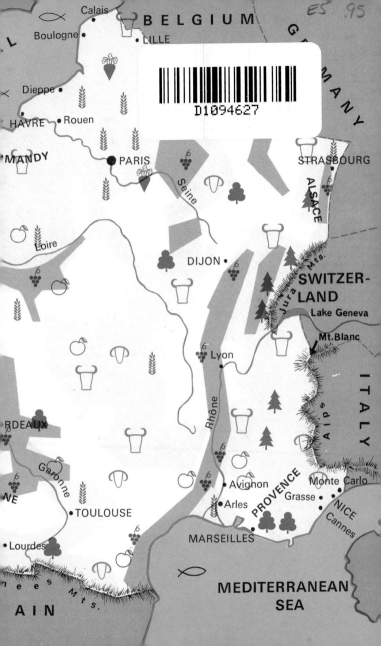

Calais

BELGIUM

Boulogne

LILLE

GERMANY

Dieppe

HAVRE

Rouen

STRASBOURG

MANDY

PARIS

ALSACE

Seine

DIJON

SWITZER-
LAND

Lake Geneva

Mt.Blanc

Loire

Jura Mts.

Lyon

Rhône

ITALY

Alps

RDEAUX

Garonne

Avignon

Monte Carlo

NE

Arles

PROVENCE

Grasse

NICE

TOULOUSE

Cannes

Lourdes

MARSEILLES

Pyrenees Mts.

MEDITERRANEAN
SEA

AIN

ES .95

D1094627

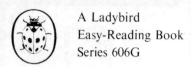

A Ladybird
Easy-Reading Book
Series 606G

This book gives an interesting and colourful glimpse of a lovely country and her people. It shows you some of the exciting things you might see if you go to France, and some of the differences in the way of life of the French people compared with your own.

A LADYBIRD 'EASY-READING' BOOK

come to
FRANCE

by IRENE DARK
with illustrations by JOHN BERRY

Publishers: Ladybird Books Ltd . Loughborough
© Ladybird Books Ltd (formerly Wills & Hepworth Ltd) 1969
Printed in England

COME TO FRANCE

France is more than twice the size of Britain and has fewer people in it. It is one of the most beautiful countries in Europe. There are very high mountains, large plains, many forests, and long rivers.

The weather in the north is very much like ours, and in the south—by the Mediterranean Sea—it is warm and sunny even in the winter. Oranges, lemons, figs and olives are grown there.

It is an exciting moment when you get your first glimpse of France. When you step from an airliner, or the gangway of a ship, you very soon know that you are not in England. All around you people are speaking rapidly in French. When you enter the nearby town, you see that all the signs and notices, posters and hoardings are in the French language.

7214 0241 0

You will have to be very careful when you cross the road in France, and your kerb drill must be the opposite of what it is in England. This is because traffic keeps to the right, so you must 'Look LEFT, look RIGHT, look LEFT again'. Do not cross the road until you have done this and made sure that the road is clear.

You will notice that the French policeman has a rather different uniform and cap from that of an English policeman. French traffic seems to hurtle past him, stop almost immediately at his command and then surge forward when he waves it on. French policemen often carry a baton and whistle.

Behind the policeman in the picture is one of the many beautiful churches and buildings in Paris, the capital of France. It was built to resemble a Roman temple.

Quite unlike any other building in France is the Eiffel Tower, the best known sight in Paris. It was built by a man named Eiffel for the World Exhibition in 1889. It was then the tallest building in the world. Even today there are very few others that are as tall.

The Tower was built almost like a huge Meccano model, and millions of nuts and bolts were used. Lifts take you to the top to enjoy the marvellous view. Near the top there is a radio and television station. Radio time signals are also sent out from there.

Everywhere in Paris there are sights worth seeing, wonderful bridges, palaces, art galleries, museums and other buildings, as well as beautiful shops.

Paris is the fourth largest city in the world. Besides all the beautiful bridges and buildings there are magnificent streets (called 'avenues' and 'boulevards') which are wide and tree-lined. Perhaps the most well-known is the Champs Elysées, which leads up to the famous arch which you can see in the picture—the Arc de Triomphe.

Inside this Arc there is a lift to the top, so that you can enjoy more views of Paris. At the foot of the Arc is the 'Eternal Flame', which burns in memory of dead soldiers of the two World Wars. At night the Arc is illuminated.

Almost every fourth shop along the Champs Elysées is a 'bistro', 'brasserie', 'café' or 'restaurant'. The citizens of Paris love to spend their evenings walking the boulevards, or sitting at the café tables, watching the people of the world go by.

Open-air cafés are part of the attractive sights of France. The tables are set out on the pavement under brightly-coloured sunshades.

Visitors to France enjoy this pleasant way of having a cup of coffee or an ice-cream. Like the French people, they enjoy sitting and watching other people passing by.

French cooking is famous all over the world. Meals are carefully prepared and served with delicious sauces. Many herbs and spices are also used.

Many French families, with their children, have their evening meal in one of the fine restaurants. The children often drink wine, with water added. France grows the grapes which make the well-known French wines.

Breakfast is a simple meal of coffee, butter and jam eaten with 'croissants', which are delicious rolls, golden brown and crescent-shaped.

Every small town in France has its open-air market. Here the local people sell their fruit and vegetables, flowers and poultry.

All French people take a special interest in good food. They come to the markets to buy it as fresh as possible. The stallholders arrange their goods well so that customers can choose from attractive displays.

The piles of melons, apricots, peaches and other fruits look delicious. Among the many vegetables you will notice lots of onions, garlic, peppers, artichokes and aubergines.

The meat stall, with its poultry and sausages, is also very clean and attractive. Best of all you will like the gay flower-stalls with their vivid bunches and sprays of many-coloured blooms.

You pay in francs for anything you buy, and its weight is measured in grammes.

Look at the map in the front of this book. You will see that France is roughly square in shape. Only a short distance separates France from Britain at the Straits of Dover. On clear days each coast line can be seen from the other side.

Britain, being an island, is surrounded by water, and you have to cross the water to get into any other country.

In France you can cross into six other countries by land. You can go over the frontier into Belgium in the north, Luxembourg, Germany, Switzerland and Italy in the east, and Spain in the south.

When you come to a Frontier Post you have to stop. Here passports are always examined, and luggage checked to prevent smuggling. Then the barrier is raised and off you go into another foreign country. At the Frontier Post you will see notices in both languages.

France has many lovely rivers. Some rush along through narrow valleys. Others flow quietly through rich meadow-land.

On the map you will see four long and important rivers of France. They are the Seine, the Loire, the Garonne, and the Rhône.

The river Seine is the best known because it flows through the centre of Paris and on to the English Channel. At its mouth is the great port of Le Havre.

Many strong and beautiful bridges cross the Seine. The suspension bridge in the picture is one of them. It is called the Tancarville Bridge.

In Paris the river is full of traffic of all kinds. A fleet of 'Bateaux Mouche' river boats takes visitors up and down the Seine, and under its thirty-nine magnificent bridges.

Normandy is a part of France which is opposite the English coast.

It is a land of farms and meadow-land. Here you will see the farms which provide the French people with milk, butter, cheese and wheat.

You may still see the old-fashioned way of milking or harvesting being used on small farms, but larger farms with very modern machinery are now becoming more general.

Many visitors to France arrive by boat at one or other of the Normandy ports. They like to spend their holidays in the seaside towns of Normandy. There are lovely, wide, sandy beaches and gay promenades with plenty of entertainments and things to do.

As you travel through the countryside, the shapes of the buildings in the villages tell you unmistakably that you are in France.

To the west of Normandy is a large piece of land which juts out into the Atlantic Ocean. Look at it on the map at the end of this book. We call this shape of land a 'peninsula'. This is Brittany. It is a part of France which is so beautiful and interesting that it attracts visitors from all over Europe. Its rugged coastline has many little seaside towns and villages.

The people who live here are called 'Bretons'. You might be lucky enough to see some of the women dressed in their national costume, with its very beautiful lace head-dress.

The Bretons are fine fishermen. Some of them fish for sardines. Sardines are caught during the night, and the boats carry large lights which shine into the water and attract the fish.

You will have to travel south to find the sort of scenery shown in the picture opposite. This is the Gascogne district. Look for it on the map.

As you go south the climate changes and becomes warmer. It also becomes very sunny. Because of this, peaches, apricots, melons and grapes grow in abundance.

Here you will again notice the old-fashioned way of farming. On the road you may meet an occasional cart creaking along. You will be surprised to see that it is being pulled by a pair of oxen.

There are many pretty villages and little towns by the sea, most of them full of holiday-makers.

One inland town, named Lourdes, is well-known to all Catholics, many of whom make a special journey there as pilgrims, some in the hope of a cure for an illness.

Another part of southern France, further to the east, is called Provence. In this area is a town called Grasse, where French perfumes have been made for hundreds of years.

All the surrounding fields seem to have carpets of flowers. There are violets in early spring, then jonquils and hyacinths.

In summer, orange-blossom and jasmine, roses and mignonette give out their delightful fragrance. These flowers are grown for the perfume factories.

Carts, full of coloured blossoms, fill the air with a trail of sweetness as they pass. If you visit one of these perfume factories, you will be able to see how the perfume of these flowers is made into the scent you can buy in tiny bottles.

It takes a lot of flowers, and a long time, to produce a very small bottle of perfume.

The coastline of Provence is on the Mediterranean Sea, and from one of France's biggest ports—Marseilles—ships sail to all parts of the world.

Provence has many old monuments, bridges and buildings. 'Sur le Pont d'Avignon' sing the children of France. You may know the English version of it too. 'Le pont' means 'the bridge', and the wonderful bridge in Avignon was built eight hundred years ago. You can still see the part of it that is standing, very old and beautiful after such a long time.

South of Avignon is the old town of Arles, where the famous artist, Van Gogh, painted so many of his pictures.

The picture opposite shows three women in the national costume of Provence, enjoying a traditional dance.

South of Arles (where the river Rhône begins to approach the sea) is an area—the Camargue—unlike anywhere else in Europe.

In early summer one sees what look like hundreds of flooded tennis lawns. These are really rice fields, with the thin blades of rice growing through the water.

Further south still in this marshy land is an area over which roam herds of half-wild bulls and white horses. The bulls are bred for fighting, but never killed in the arena. Instead, young men compete to snatch ribbons from a bull's head.

The herds of animals are tended by herdsmen who look and live like cowboys.

One part of this south coast of France is called 'The Playground of Europe'. It has lovely sunshine, many fine sandy beaches and very beautiful scenery. It is perfect for a holiday. People who have enough money, like to go and live there.

Along the coast are seaside resorts that are famous—Cannes, Monte Carlo (in the independent state of Monaco) and Nice. They are full of hotels—magnificent, expensive and like palaces.

Yachts of all kinds are moored in the many harbours. These vary from small racing boats to the large yachts of millionaires.

The promenades are lined with palm trees, and flowers are everywhere.

Life is very gay at carnival time, with its Battle of Flowers and amusing processions of floats, built up with grotesque and colourful figures.

A journey to Lake Geneva will take you into very different country. To get there you must pass through the Alps, the highest mountain range in Europe. The south bank of this lovely lake is in France and the north bank is in Switzerland.

The highest peak in the Alps is in France. It is called Mont Blanc (the White Mountain) and is three and a half times as high as Ben Nevis in Scotland. Once you have seen it, you will never forget its striking shape and great beauty. At the foot of Mont Blanc is the holiday resort of Chamonix. Here, as well as at other places in the French Alps, people come in winter for ski-ing and skating. In summer they come for climbing, or to enjoy the wonderful scenery.

You will sometimes see ski-lifts in these mountainous spots. They are little carriages slung on overhead wires, which carry people high up into the mountains.

The people of Alsace wear their national costumes with great pride. These costumes are very beautiful and often hand-made. One generation hands them on to the next. In the picture you can also see one of the old and attractive Alsatian houses.

If you travel north from the Alps, you will arrive at a part of France which has a frontier with Germany. The great river Rhine is the boundary now between these two countries.

This region of farms and vineyards sends famous wines to many other countries. Not far away, in the Jura district, is the home of the Gruyère cheese which you may have sometimes on your table at home. France is famous for its cheeses.

Strasbourg, a large and very old town, has many fine and ancient buildings as well as important engineering industries. Its magnificent cathedral is well worth seeing.

Wherever you go in France, you are likely to see vineyards where grapes are grown with great skill to be made into wine. France is the world's most important producer of wine. Each district grows its own kind of grapes, which gives the wine a different taste from that of other districts. Many of the wines are called by the name of the place where they are produced.

This is the kind of scene you will see at harvest time. The sun is very hot, and often the womenfolk wear large sunbonnets that protect their heads and faces from the burning sun.

The grapes are loaded onto trucks which take them away to the wine distilleries, to be made into one or other of the famous wines of France.

'Château' is the French word for castle, but castles in France are not quite the same in appearance as those in Britain. Some of them were fortified, but most of them are great houses built in olden days by kings, princes and noblemen, and where they lived in luxury.

The valley of the river Loire has many châteaux and thousands of visitors go to see them.

Each château has its own special shape and architecture. Some are built in or near an old town, which has grown up around it. Some are built along the riverside. One château, called Chenonceaux, is known for its famous gallery built over the river.

Those which have tall, round towers rising to a point, look like fairy-tale castles. After dark, when they are floodlit, they seem to float in the air like fairy palaces.

Long before fast motorways were built by other countries, France had many trunk roads. They spread out from Paris like the spokes of a wheel.

These are called the Routes Nationales. They are very busy with the traffic of cars, and large lorries with just as large trailers. Most of this traffic goes right through France into other countries in Europe. Every kilometre is marked along the route.

There are other roads, too, which stay in the mind of the visitor. They are usually very straight, and planted with tall trees, like poplars. These form beautiful avenues which stretch for hundreds of kilometres. The picture shows one of the smaller country roads between quiet villages and smaller market towns.

Paris is not only the centre of the French road system; from this great city also radiate the waterways and most of the main railway lines.

Boats and barges carry goods to and from French factories and ports, and can travel along rivers and canals for hundreds of kilometres.

These railway lines and waterways are thickest in the north-east—around the town of Lille—where there are the biggest coal mines, and many factories.

France is proud of the punctuality and speed of her trains. The world speed record was gained by a French locomotive, which reached more than three hundred and twenty-eight kilometres an hour.

Like other great cities, Paris also has its own airport, where international aircraft take off and land.

Many British visitors travel to France by ship, and land at one of her Channel ports, at Calais, Boulogne, Dieppe, Le Havre, Cherbourg or St. Malo.

The most important of these is Le Havre, at the mouth of the river Seine. This picture shows you the French liner, S.S. France —the longest in the world—as she is moored alongside a quay there.

These ports are very busy, as many passengers and much goods traffic pass to and from other countries. The docks have many warehouses for goods which have been brought by lorry, train or barge, ready to be put in ships, or which have been unloaded from them.

Through Le Havre come supplies of cotton from America, and wool from Australia and New Zealand. These go to Rouen and other towns in the north and east of France, where they are made into cloth. Rouen is often called the 'Manchester of France'.

In the Alps, and wherever there is fast flowing water, large dams are built to hold it back so that the flowing water can be used to drive turbines. These turn generators to make electricity, which is taken by cables to works and factories, towns and villages.

Now a new way of getting electricity has been found. A dam has been built in the mouth of a river. The sea flows in with the rising tide, and the water is held by the dam and used to make electricity.

Britain and France help each other with their supplies of electricity. They are linked by undersea cables so that each can borrow from the other when needed.

This is a picture of one of these hydro-electric power stations, as they are called.

Bicycle racing is a well-loved sport in France. There are many local races, but for most French people the most important event is the 'Tour de France'. This race lasts for twenty to twenty-five days in summer. Racers come from all over the world to compete. They have to ride along the roads that go all round the edge of France. They have to pedal along under scorching skies, and climb mountain passes hundreds of metres high. They face the risk of many accidents, such as being bumped by another racer or even falling down cliffs.

An ambulance helicopter follows the race in case of such accidents. At the end of each 'lap' the riders sleep in the town they have reached.

The next morning everyone turns out to cheer them on their way. The race ends in Paris amid great excitement.

INDUSTRY

France is a leading industrial country, being the third largest producer of iron ore in the world and the sixth largest in the production of steel.

---

 mining

hydro-electric schemes

petrol

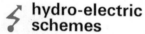 engineering industry

chemical industry

ENGLAND

ENGLISH CH

ENGLISH

Cherb

Brest

St. M

BRITTANY

ATLANTIC OCEAN